For Isabelle and Chloe

A Walk to the Cloud
by Mitch and Elyse Seymour

Text copyright © 2022 Round Robin Publishing
Illustrations copyright © 2022 Round Robin Publishing

All rights reserved. This book or any portion thereof may not be reproduced or used in any manner whatsoever without the express written permission of the publisher except for the use of brief quotations in a book review.

First printing, 2022.

Round Robin Publishing
www.roundrobin.pub

 hello@roundrobin.pub

A Walk to the Cloud

by Mitch and Elyse Seymour

It was monsoon season in the forest, and no matter how hard the otters tried, they couldn't keep the wind out.

It blew away their hats, it blew away their picnic blankets, but worst of all, it made the great Kafka river run wild and fierce.

The otters had been using the Kafka river to communicate with each other, floating messages down streams about various events happening in the forest.

It worked really well, but occasional bad weather made the river difficult to manage.

In addition to bad weather, the otters spent a lot of time worrying about the amount of water in the Kafka river.

If the river had too little water, the otters would have trouble storing all of their messages. Too much water would be wasteful and inefficient. This meant the otters had to do **Capacity Planning** to make sure the river always had the right amount of water.

To cope with these challenges, the otters kept a close eye on the forest and river. They actively monitored the weather, collected data about their environment, and tailed the logs.

Tailing the logs just means an otter parks their tail on a log, and watches for Signs of Trouble as the day goes by.

The otters also worried about other creatures looking at their messages in the river.

If the bees knew what the otters were saying about them, they would have a Real Security Problem on their hands. So, they spent a lot of time and energy securing the river from outside threats.

No bees were harmed during the making of this book

All of this extra work created **Operational Overhead** for the otters. Most otters didn't care for this extra work, because it took time away from what they really wanted to do: swim and communicate in the river.

Then, on one especially blustery day (some say it was a Winds day, but I wouldn't go that far), it was Nixie's turn to tail the logs.

As she sat on the river bank, drifting off between bursts of rain, a wild gust of wind blew under her umbrella and carried her westerly toward the Cloud Forests.

When the wind finally ran out of breath, she found herself in the tree of a spotted cat-like creature, who looked curiously at the tired and wet otter.

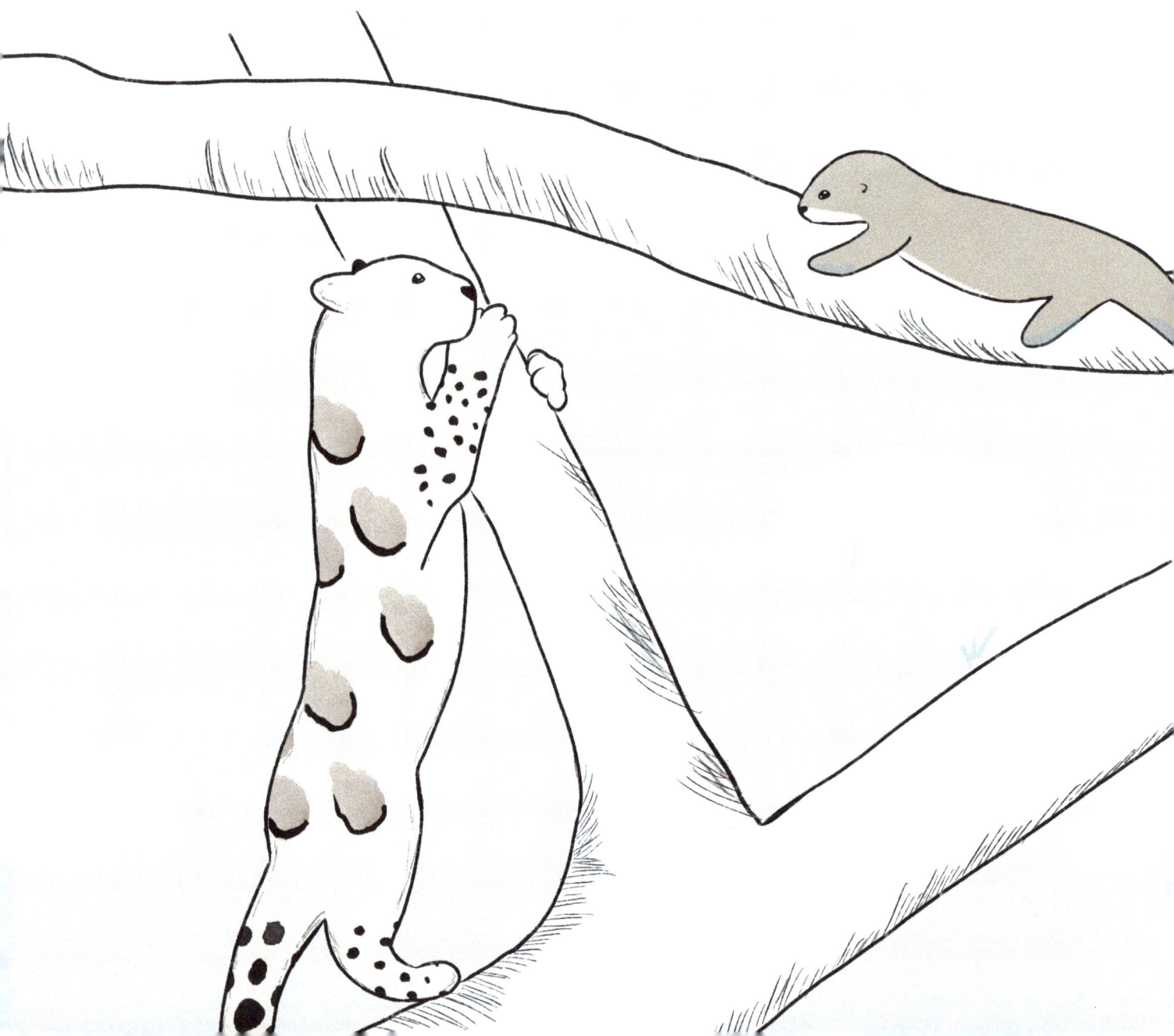

Nixie thought the creature must be an Ocelot, since it was too big to be an Ocelittle, and too friendly to be a Tiger. But before Nixie could introduce herself, the creature said:

I'm Purja the Clouded Leopard

Nixie introduced herself, and explained how the Unpredictable Winds had riled up the river back home, and how the winds had carried her right into Purja's tree.

Purja thought quietly for a minute, and then said "there is a place beyond the mountains, where the rivers are larger, calmer, and more secure. The place is called **The Cloud**, and your life will be easier there."

Having never heard of rivers in clouds, Nixie asked if Purja would take her there. The Kafka river back home had become difficult to manage, and she hoped she'd find answers in this mysterious place. Purja agreed, and the two began their journey.

As they crossed the first bridge toward the mountains, Nixie asked Purja, "what makes The Cloud so special?"

"You don't have to worry about the environment when you're in The Cloud", Purja said, "others will manage it for you. These are called **Fully Managed Environments**, and they free you up to do more interesting things with your time".

"So the otters will have more time to swim and communicate in the river?". "That's right", Purja said. "And where exactly are the fully managed environments?" Nixie asked.

Just as Purja was about to answer, they came to a ridge that overlooked several mountains, each one enveloped in a large, swirling cloud.

"There are several ecosystems, called **Clouds**," Purja said.

"Clouds are Very Big Places, and contain fully managed environments and other resources that will make your life easier.

The blue ecosystem over there is Microsoft Azure, the one covered in green moss is Amazon Web Services, and the one with the colorful banner is called Google Cloud Platform. There are other Clouds, as well, but those are the biggest."

"You can go to any **Cloud Provider** and they will help you find a cloud environment in their ecosystem, and some of these environments will be fully managed.

"You can also have a river in multiple clouds if you don't want to be tied down to a single ecosystem. This is called a **Multi-cloud** strategy, and it gives you the most flexibility."

As they got closer to the mountains, Nixie noticed that some of the clouds looked a little different. There seemed to be different types of clouds available from each Cloud Provider.

"What is the cloud that everyone seems to be sharing over there?"

"That's a **Public Cloud.**"

"And what about the cloud that is fenced off for only that small group of animals?"

"That's a **Private Cloud.**"

Just then, the little gray rain cloud started to sprinkle, and Nixie immediately thought back to her own river.

The otters had sometimes conserved extra rainwater in case the river needed more water to store their messages.

Adding extra storage capacity by hand was called **Manually Scaling**. It helped the otters store more messages in the river, but it was a tedious task and not very effiicient.

Nixie asked Purja how scaling worked for rivers in The Cloud. Fortunately, the two happened to be passing by a small dwelling, where some little yellow bears were blowing up balloons for a birthday party.

Purja picked up a balloon, and said "scaling in The Cloud works like this balloon." He puffed a big breath of air into the balloon, and Nixie watched it get bigger.

"The air in the balloon represents the work you have to do, and also your data. It's your workload. When your workload gets bigger, your river will *automatically* get bigger too, just like the balloon.

This is called **Scaling Up**."

Then, Purja let some of the air out of the balloon, and said, "Similarly, when your workload gets smaller, your river will automatically get smaller, too.

This is called **Scaling Down**, and the process of automatically scaling up and down like a balloon is called **Elastic Scaling**. This is how we scale workloads in The Cloud".

"What if the air, I mean - our data, gets too big?", Nixed asked. "Will the balloon pop?"

"For certain kinds of cloud rivers, the data can never be too big, and you'll never have to worry about losing it.

This is called **Infinite Storage and Retention.** It's something that many Cloud Natives need.

Looking at the little bears, Nixie whispered "are they Cloud Natives?"

Purja laughed, and said "Anything that is designed to make the most of The Cloud's features, like fully managed environments, elastic scaling, and high availability, is said to be **Cloud Native**."

The two friends kept walking.

They crossed a wet log, a narrow ridge, and two sparkling snow hills before finally arriving at the foot of the mountains. As they approached, Nixie heard the familiar roar of the Kafka river.

This river was very similar to the one back home - with lots of streams, places for **Producers** to put messages in, and places for **Consumers** to read those same messages. However, it was much larger and in much better shape than the river she left behind.

"What is this place?" she asked.

"This is the place where the rivers and clouds meet. We call it **Confluent Cloud**." Purja said. Here, a special group of otters will help you manage a Kafka river in any cloud environment you want.

Nixie saw a lot of otters managing the river, actively cleaning it, scaling it, and securing it from bees and other Threatening Creatures. It had everything Purja had promised: elastic scalability, infinite storage, and security.

In fact, all of the boring operational work that Nixie had been spending so much time on back home was already taken care of in Confluent Cloud.

She looked up at Purja, who was starting to turn away back toward his home. "These Kafka rivers are fully managed, Nixie. The only thing left to do is jump in and get your feet wet. Play and communicate. And build things in the river knowing that it's a safe and scalable environment."

goodbye Nixie

And so that's what Nixie did. She jumped in the river and loved it so much that she brought her entire otter family to The Cloud to play in it, as well. The otters never had to worry about their environment again, and they lived happily ever after.

Vocabulary 🌸

Capacity planning	A tedious task of deciding how many resources you need.
Cloud	An ecosystem of services or resources.
• Public cloud	• A cloud that is shared across multiple groups.
• Private cloud	• A cloud that is dedicated to a single group.
• Hybrid cloud	• A cloud that combines both public and private clouds.
• Multi-cloud	• When multiple clouds are used for a specific task / resource.
Cloud native	Anything that is designed to take full advantage of The Cloud's strengths (e.g. high availability, elastic scalability, etc).
Cloud provider	A company (e.g. Amazon, Google, Microsoft) that shares their Clouds with other people.
Fully managed environments	An environment where others manage the resources for you.
Ocelittle	A small Ocelot.
Operational overhead	Difficulties that often come with self-managed environments.
Scalability	The ability to handle different amounts of work gracefully.
• Elastic scaling	• The process of scaling up **and** down, like a balloon.
• Manual scaling	• A time-consuming process of scaling resources by hand.
• Scaling up	• Adding more resources to handle lots of work.
• Scaling down	• Removing resources when there's less work to do.

www.ingramcontent.com/pod-product-compliance
Lightning Source LLC
LaVergne TN
LVHW071958060526
838200LV00010B/234